MONSTERS & CREATURES

DUNGEONS & DRAGONS®

MONSTERS &
CREATURES

A Young Adventurer's Guide

WRITTEN BY JIM ZUB

WITH STACY KING AND ANDREW WHEELER

TEN SPEED PRESS
California | New York

CONTENTS

INTRODUCTION

Monsters are freaky. Creatures can be fun. Both make our stories exciting and dangerous.

This book is a tour through some of the most famous and frightening beasts from the world of DUNGEONS & DRAGONS. It's a guide to their traits, lairs, and powers. It will tell you how to fight these weird creatures or advise you when to flee if you're in over your head.

Read this book from start to finish, or open it to any spot, get entranced by the cool artwork, and start your journey there. The more you read, the more you'll discover. The more you discover, the easier it will be to imagine your own heroic tales as you explore strange caves, trek across craggy mountains, or soar through the skies.

Will your battles against these monsters lead to fame and fortune or will your skeleton lie as an omen for future heroes to discover? In the end, that's up to you. DUNGEONS & DRAGONS is all about unique adventures, and yours is about to begin.

Enjoy!

DANGER LEVELS

Each monster profile includes a number indicating the danger level of that creature, with a **0** being harmless, a **1** as a reasonable threat for a beginning adventurer, and building up from there. A **5** is incredibly dangerous and requires an experienced group of adventurers to possibly defeat it. There are some **epic** creatures more powerful than a mere number can define. Such terrors can only be fought by legendary heroes armed with the most powerful magic weapons and spells imaginable.

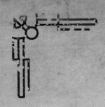

CAVERNS & DARK PLACES

In the earth beneath your feet, things are *moving*.

Creatures of all shapes and sizes burrow through dirt and stone, muck and clay. Vast tunnels connect to winding caves, and inside those flow rivers that have never seen the sun. In places such as the Underdark, entire kingdoms of intelligent creatures can be found.

Some of these subterranean spaces are cool and wet, with condensation dripping from above. Others are hot and steamy, with a thin wall of rock serving as your only protection from streams of burning magma that bubble up from a molten core.

The underground is a place of darkness and danger, where hidden treasures can be found in a hole and a sputtering torch is your only source of light. Are you ready to go exploring?

BEHOLDER

4

SPECIAL POWERS Beholders have one big eyeball in the center of their round bodies and ten weird eyestalks. Each eyestalk has a magic beam that shoots at adventurers when angry.

TELEKINESIS
This eye's beam can hold you in place or move you around.

ENERVATION
This eye's spell hurts like a bad burn.

SLOWNESS
If this eye's beam hits you, then you'll move really slowly, like you're trying to run underwater.

FEAR
If this eye's spell works its magic, you'll find yourself running away because of uncontrollable fear.

PARALYZATION
If you get hit with this one, you won't be able to move at all for a full minute. Count to sixty and hope you still have time to run afterward.

DISINTEGRATION
This eye's beam turns whatever it hits to dust.

SLEEP
This eye's beam can make you so tired that you fall asleep on the spot. No pillow. No blanket. Just naptime.

PETRIFICATION
One hit from this eye's beam will turn a living creature into stone.

DEATH
Yikes!

CHARM
If you fall under this eye's spell, you'll think the beholder is your friend and do what it says.

ANTIMAGIC CONE
Wherever this eye looks, magic won't work. Clerics, wizards, and warlocks, try to stay out of its sight.

Beholders are freaky floating creatures with shimmering eyes that cast evil spells. Is that big blob the beholder's head or its body? Are those eyestalks coming out of the top its hair or its limbs? There are no easy answers. All you need to know is that a beholder is a scary floating eyeball monster. And if any of those eyes set their gaze on you, you're in big trouble.

Beholders are jealous, angry creatures. They have such a bad attitude that they don't even get along with each other (which is actually a good thing because if you found more than one at the same time you'd probably be a goner).

LAIR Most beholders live in remote places such as caves or abandoned ruins. Some of them even build their own lairs by disintegrating rock with their eye blasts in order to create tall tunnels where they can float above their prey and cause trouble. The floor of a beholder's cave is usually covered with treasure and equipment from unfortunate adventurers who didn't think to look up when they walked in the entrance.

SIZE Some beholders are small like a basketball, but older ones can be massive, more than ten feet in diameter, like a humongous beachball.

DO THIS

Fight magic with magic. If your party includes spellcasters, get them to put up magical shields to protect your fighters from the beholder's eye beams.

Distract the beholder as much as you can. Give it a lot of different things to look at so that it won't see you.

Get in close! Beholders are most dangerous when they're far away because they can shoot their eye beams at you and your party.

DON'T DO THIS

Don't ignore the feeling that you're being watched. Even when you're alone, feeling someone's eyes on you is a sign that a beholder may be close by.

Don't stay put for too long! Holding your ground may be a great fighting tactic against some monsters, but not against beholders. If those eyes focus on you, it's bad news.

BUGBEAR

1

SPECIAL POWERS

BRUTE STRENGTH
Close combat weapons do extra damage when wielded by these ferocious fighters.

HEART OF HRUGGEK
Named after a bugbear god, bugbear chiefs can call upon this formidable power to shrug off attacks intended to charm, frighten, paralyze, poison, or stun them.

SURPRISE ATTACK
An explosive burst of power allows a bugbear to inflict even more damage during its first strike, raising its danger level, if It manages to catch you off guard.

SIZE Bugbears are a little taller than a normal doorway, with broad shoulders and thick, muscular limbs. Their abnormally long arms give them extra reach for melee attacks.

Bugbears are fierce warriors born for battle and mayhem! Much larger than their goblin cousins (see page 12), bugbears like to bully and boss other creatures around. They will fight for others if their employer promises enough gold and carnage to satisfy their barbaric tastes. However, even a well-paid bugbear is an unreliable ally. Covered in thick fur that they enhance with hide armor, they favor brutal weapons such as the morning star, a spiked mace.

Bugbears are fond of ambushes and are surprisingly stealthy for their size. They are often found in the company of goblins whom they have enslaved or rule over with brutal force (though they do sometimes unite to form war bands led by a particularly strong warrior). Beneath their fierce exteriors, bugbears are cowards who will abandon wounded members of their parties and flee when the fight turns against them. A wounded bugbear has no qualms about betraying his former allies if it will help save his own hide!

LAIR Like goblins, bugbears favor dismal settings such as caves, abandoned mines, and rotting dungeons. Some simply move into goblin lairs and take over! You may sometimes find war bands rampaging through rocky terrain or anywhere that treasure and conquests can be found.

DO THIS	DON'T DO THIS
Stay out of reach. Bugbears' long arms give them an advantage in close combat, so use ranged attacks when possible.	**Don't ignore their goblin companions.** The smaller creatures may be less dangerous one-on-one, but a goblin horde presents a risk for even the most accomplished adventurer.
Take captives. Bugbears will sell out their tribe and allies for a chance at survival.	**Don't let down your guard.** Known for their stealth, bugbears love to attack when they're least expected. Stay alert!

CARRION CRAWLER

SPECIAL POWERS

SENSE OF SMELL
Carrion crawlers have an amazing sense of smell that lets them sniff out prey from far away. That also makes it tough to sneak up on them.

CLIMBING
Their many legs allow them to climb like a spider, skittering over difficult surfaces and even moving while upside down.

POISON
Their tentacles carry a poison that can paralyze you. Once you can't move, the carrion crawler will tuck you away to let you die and rot until you're gooey enough to be its next meal.

Carrion crawlers are huge caterpillar-like creatures, each with dozens of tentacles and a gnashing mouth full of razor-sharp teeth. These disgusting monsters live on rotting flesh and slimy bones, and they're always on the hunt for their next meal.

Carrion crawlers are drawn to dead things. They follow the stench of death and decay like relentless bloodhounds. These patient predators rely on trickery to fill their ever-hungry bellies. Unwary adventurers face the risk of being grabbed and poisoned by one of their many tentacles or bitten by their snapping teeth.

LAIR Carrion crawlers are found in caves, sewers, dungeons, and marshlands—anywhere that's dark and moldy. Their keen sense of smell can sometimes lead them to cemeteries or battlefields. The dark corners of their lairs may contain the paralyzed or rotting corpses of their victims, stashed away for a late-night snack.

SIZE A fully grown carrion crawler is three times as long as a human is tall and almost six feet high when they crawl around. However, they can rear up on their hind-tentacles in combat to make themselves even taller, so watch out!

DO THIS	DON'T DO THIS
Be ready to cure poisonous wounds. Party members with healing powers, like clerics and druids, should be ready to help if anyone is struck by a poisonous tentacle.	**Don't make lots of noise while you move through the underground.** These relentless hunters will stalk you for hours in hopes of a meal.
Clean your weapons after a fight. Carrion crawlers can smell even a tiny hint of blood from miles away.	**Don't ignore what's above.** Carrion crawlers can move across ceilings just as easily as they can the ground, and they love to surprise their victims from above.

FLUMPH

SPECIAL POWERS

ADVANCED TELEPATHY
These powerful psychics can overhear the content of any telepathic communication within sixty feet.

TELEPATHIC SHROUD
Flumphs are immune to all attempts to read their thoughts or emotions against their will.

STENCH SPRAY
Flumphs can shoot a fifteen-foot-long cone of foul-smelling liquid that sticks to targets, leaving them stinking for hours.

ACID BURN
Flumphs can attack with their tendrils, which give off an acid that can burn skin.

Not everything that lurks in the dark is dangerous! Flumphs are one of the great oddities of the underground, peaceful little creatures who float through the darkness on puffs of air. They communicate telepathically and express their moods through the soft, glowing colors of their tentacles: soft pink for amusement, deep blue for sadness, green for curiosity, and red for anger.

Flumphs feed off the psychic energy of others. They are passive parasites who take only as much as needed for survival. Their telepathy exposes them to the evil thoughts and emotions of other underground dwellers, sickening their pure nature. When good-hearted adventurers approach, flumphs are eager to soak up the positive energy and share any dark secrets they have learned. A steadfast rule of underground exploration is to always trust a flumph!

LAIR Flumphs live in the Underdark and can typically be found near the lairs of mind flayers and other psionic creatures. Their own communities, called cloisters, are peaceful places where their telepathy allows them to live in perfect harmony.

SIZE An adult flumph has a circumference wider than a person, but is only about as thick as your arm, giving it an odd and flat saucer-shaped appearance.

DO THIS	DON'T DO THIS
Let them into your head. Flumphs can't speak, but they can share secrets and warnings via telepathy.	**Don't frighten them.** Dungeons are stinky enough without being coated with a flumph's stench spray.
Keep an eye on their colors. Flumphs are angered by the presence of evil, so when they start to glow red, something bad is nearby.	

GOBLIN

GOBLIN POLITICS

Lairs are ruled by the strongest or smartest goblin, who must constantly fight to hold their position. Turnover among goblin bosses is high, since all goblins want to seize power for themselves! Many goblin tribes are ruled by bugbears (see page 6), who use their superior strength and size to bully their smaller cousins into submission.

SIZE Goblins are about the height of a kitchen table. They are short but stocky, which gives them better balance when moving across rocky or uneven terrain.

Goblins are small, black-hearted, and selfish creatures with an individually low danger rating—which is why they're almost always found in packs, often in numbers so great that they can simply overwhelm their enemies! These malicious creatures long for power and cannot help but celebrate whenever they have the upper hand. Lazy and undisciplined, they make poor servants and rely on alarms rather than guards to protect their lairs.

Goblins have an affinity for rats, which serve as pets, and wolves, whom they train as mounts. They prefer ambushes and hit-and-run attacks over straightforward battle. When alone, they are more likely to run away than challenge a stronger foe—but they can be dangerous when they band together! Goblins fight with scimitars and shortbows, and wear leather armor stolen from fallen enemies. Even with a leader, their infighting never stops. Goblins live to abuse, and they will turn on one another if no external target is available (a trait that adventurers can use to their advantage).

LAIR You'll find goblins in old caves, abandoned mines, derelict dungeons, and other forsaken places. They take advantage of their small size by riddling their lairs with tunnels and bolt-holes that block the passage of larger enemies. Goblins also set many traps and alarms to ensure they aren't caught unaware.

DO THIS

Target the leader. Goblins are cowardly and often run away once their strongest fighter is defeated.

Stay alert! Goblins favor ambushes and sneak attacks from behind, so beware when traveling through their territories.

Put on a fearsome show. Sometimes all it takes is a magic illusion or a powerful battle cry to send them scurrying.

DON'T DO THIS

Don't rush into battle. Goblin lairs are riddled with traps and alarms. Be careful to avoid setting them off.

Don't trust them! Goblins are habitual liars and cannot be trusted to keep their promises (unless their lives are on the line).

MIND FLAYER

3

SPECIAL POWERS

DOMINATE MONSTER
Overpowers the mind of any living creature, turning them into a psychic slave willing to give their own life for their master.

BRAIN EXTRACTION
A mighty attack, which works against already-stunned foes, allows the mind flayer to crack open enemy skulls and devour their brains.

MIND BLAST
A psychic attack that batters heroes with powerful mental energy, leaving them stunned.

PSYCHIC STRIKE
Their tentacles can deliver damaging blows using psychic power and snare you in a tight grasp.

SIZE Adult mind flayers are only slightly larger than normal humans. (It's their psychic powers, not their size, that make them deadly!) Elder brains are around ten feet in diameter.

Wherever they appear, mind flayers are the scourge of sentient creatures. Psychic overlords and slavers, they are sinister masterminds that will not hesitate to wipe out entire races to achieve their own evil ends. Once, their empires oppressed many worlds; even today, their mental powers allow them to enact far-reaching schemes of intense cruelty.

The four tentacles on the squidlike head of a mind flayer are channels for their psychic powers. Mind flayers communicate telepathically, both among themselves and with the creatures they have psychically enslaved. Solitary mind flayers are rare, as most belong to colonies, each of which serves an elder brain. When a loyal mind flayer dies, its brain is harvested and deposited in the briny pool where the elder brain resides, so their gray matter and knowledge can be absorbed by their leader. A mind flayer's mental control is so absolute that their slaves will battle to the death to protect their master!

LAIR Mind flayers reside within the Underdark, a vast network of subterranean tunnels and caves that lies below the earth. They live in colonies of five or more adults who are all related to the elder brain that lives in a briny pool near the middle of their den. Mind flayers acting alone are outcasts, and often gather mind-controlled slaves around themselves for added security.

DO THIS

Aim for the brain. Despite its impressive mental attacks, the elder brain is relatively defenseless compared to an adult mind flayer.

Watch out for others. Mind flayers rarely live alone, so look out for siblings or enslaved creatures.

Starve them out. Mind flayers eat humanoid brains to survive. Cut off their food supply to weaken them before your final attack.

DON'T DO THIS

Don't focus on their slaves. If you can kill the mind flayer, you'll break its control—and freed slaves are more likely to run than continue attacking.

Don't let down your guard. It will take all of your focus not to fall prey to the mind flayer's psychic powers.

MYCONID

1

SPECIAL POWERS

DISTRESS SPORES

When hurt, a myconid releases special spores that alert other myconids within two hundred forty feet of its pain.

PACIFYING SPORES

These spores can stun a single target near the myconid, allowing the pacifist creature to avoid combat.

RAPPORT SPORES

All creatures within a thirty-foot radius are bound together in a telepathic link that allows them to communicate silently for one hour.

ANIMATING SPORES

Produced by myconid sovereigns, these spores reanimate the corpses of living creatures, transforming them into loyal servants.

SIZE

SPROUT

All myconids begin life as sprouts, two to three feet tall, which gradually grow to adult size. They are relatively defenseless, but capable of wielding small melee weapons.

ADULT

Adults are six- to seven-foot-tall plant creatures capable of defending themselves with pacifying spores that stun opponents.

SOVEREIGN

At more than ten feet tall, these are the largest of all myconids. Sovereigns can reanimate dead creatures to do their bidding!

Myconids are intelligent, mobile fungi who resemble mushrooms, if mushrooms were shaped sort of like humans. These strange, intelligent creatures live in a sprawling subterranean kingdom called the Underdark, seeking enlightenment through communal mind-melds they create using their specialized spores.

If approached peacefully, myconids will allow adventurers safe passage through their colonies. They dislike violence, but are more than capable of defending themselves if attacked. Their spores can create psychic connections with other creatures and signal distress, induce calm, and even—in the case of their mighty sovereigns—reanimate the bodies of small- to large-size creatures. These loyal spore servants will not hesitate to defend their myconid masters from intruding adventurers, so be careful!

LAIR Myconids live in the Underdark and have darkvision, which allows them to move freely through the inky blackness of their homes. Each colony is made up of twenty or so myconid adults and a handful of their child sprouts, overseen by a powerful sovereign who is the largest in the colony.

DO THIS

Ask for help! These peaceful, intelligent creatures can be useful allies, sharing valuable knowledge of the area around their colony and the dangers that lie ahead.

Let the sunshine in! As dwellers of the Underdark, myconids can be weakened and even killed by exposure to sunlight. Maybe your party's magic-users have a spell that could help light up the darkness!

DON'T DO THIS

Don't think that a scarf over your nose will save you! Spores can be absorbed through the smallest patch of bare skin.

Don't brag about your conquests. Myconids despise violence!

MYCONID COLONY

Tulra shivered as the strange spores settled into her skin. Everything about the Underdark was unsettling, but the myconid colonies, with their eerie silence and musty, alien smells, were her least favorite. Still, the myconids had insight into the mind flayer known as Deenarh—knowledge she needed if she was to have any hope of breaking its dark hold over her village.

A shudder ran along Tulra's spine as the spores did their work, opening her up to the thoughts of the creatures around her. A dozen minds sparkled along the telepathic link, one brighter than the rest.

"We know you, barbarian," said the sovereign, its voice nothing but a psychic rattle in Tulra's head. "You smell like the half-orc who burnt down our colonies at Shilmista three summers past."

Tulra froze. The power of the myconid mind-meld was legendary, but she hadn't expected to be identified hundreds of miles from Shilmista. The revelation left her with a difficult choice. She could explain the terrible situation that led to the colony's demise and hope for forgiveness or lie and say it wasn't her—a difficult task given the psychic bond that linked their minds together.

Should Tulra tell a dangerous truth or a dangerous lie? If she chooses the truth, would the myconid colony offer her forgiveness or use their dangerous spores to seek revenge? If she lies, will the myconids detect her deception—and how would they react to discovering her untruth? It's up to you!

DEMOGORGON

EPIC

SPECIAL POWERS Demogorgon can use his huge tentacles or tail to grab heroes and smash them. He can also cast powerful magic spells, but his most potent abilities come from the glowing eyes of his twin ape heads. With just a glance, Demogorgon can cause heroes to stop in their tracks or go crazy.

BEGUILING GAZE
Stuns you so you can't move or think as long as you're staring at him.

HYPNOTIC GAZE
Lets Demogorgon take control, making you do whatever he chooses if your mind isn't strong enough to resist.

INSANITY GAZE
Unravels your mind so your thoughts don't make any sense. Confused and dizzy, you won't be able to attack or communicate with anyone else.

Demogorgon is a horrific demon prince who epitomizes the forces of chaos. His massive body is a warped mixture of different creatures all jammed together: the legs, feet, and tail of a dinosaur; the tentacles of a giant octopus; and the upper body of an ape, with a pair of disturbing-looking apelike heads mounted on top, hungry and roaring. Demogorgon is one of the most dangerous creatures anywhere. A battle with him is either the well-planned culmination of a massive quest, or a suicidal fool's run that ends in annihilation.

Demogorgon embodies madness and destruction, and he constantly works to destroy order and goodness in the universe. The turmoil around Demogorgon helps empower him, but it's also a source of weakness. His two heads (named Aameul and Hathradiah) constantly argue about how best to destroy his foes, as his evil plans shift and change. It's hard to raise an army and plunge the world into chaos when your own two heads can rarely agree on how best to do it.

LAIR Demogorgon lives in a strange other dimension called the Abyss. The Abyss is a shifting and turbulent place of war and insanity, where only the most powerful adventurers could even have a chance to survive, let alone triumph. The Abyss is broken up into more than six hundred layers of dangerous lands, some of them without any ground to walk on, others without any air to breathe. On the Abyssal layer called the Gaping Maw, Demogorgon's fortress is partially submerged in dark and deadly water.

Traveling to the Abyss and confronting Demogorgon directly is almost impossible for anyone less than the most epic of heroes. Most battles with Demogorgon take place elsewhere, when the Prince of Demons chooses to travel to other worlds.

SIZE Demogorgon is eighteen feet tall, which means he could look into the second-story window of a multistory house. Each of his tentacles is wider than your whole body, and his ape mouths are large enough to bite you in half without even chewing.

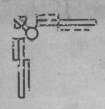

FORESTS, MOUNTAINS & OTHER TERRAIN

Open fields. Gentle hills. Quiet forests. These are the lands where many people make their homes, living peaceful lives of farming and trade, communities large and small connected by interweaving roads.

But people are not the only ones who flock to such terrain. Rocky hills and shallow caves provide promising lairs for brutal beasts. Roadside obstructions allow ambushers to set upon unwary travelers. Even open plains may make a suitable home for the clever and the quick.

Though open sky may feel less oppressive than the claustrophobic dark of an underground lair, the creatures who prowl beneath the sun and stars are no less dangerous than the subterranean variety. Are you prepared to take on monsters who threaten the safety of peaceful communities across the land?

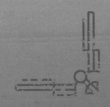

CENTAUR

THE WISDOM OF CENTAURS You might never encounter centaurs out in the wild, as they prefer to travel through remote lands. However, if they are too old or weak to travel, a lone centaur may end up living in a humanoid settlement. These noble individuals are often revered in the community for their knowledge of the world and ability to read natural omens.

SIZE The horse part of a centaur is about the same size and height of a large and powerful horse, but the human half of a centaur adds to its overall height, making these very imposing creatures to face in battle.

The proud nomadic race of creatures known as centaurs combine the speed and strength of horses with the determination and intelligence of humans. Their upper bodies allow them to wield weapons for hunting or warfare, while their lower bodies allow them to traverse great distances at tremendous speed or to trample an enemy underfoot.

Centaurs are tribal creatures who move along the same ancient trading routes used for generations, through lush forests, snow-capped mountains, and dry deserts, capturing or trading whatever supplies they need as they go. As they have no territory to defend, they are not naturally inclined toward war, but they still train for it, and are powerful and ferocious warriors when crossed.

Yet centaurs prefer a peaceful life, living in harmony with nature. They have tremendous respect for the cycles of the natural world, taking only what they need and giving back what they can.

LAIR Centaurs do not have lairs. They only settle in one place when forced to do so by injury or age. If you encounter a group of centaurs by an oasis or a lake one day, they will be gone the next, leaving little behind except hoofprints in the mud.

DO THIS

Keep your distance. Centaurs do not enjoy company, and they can strike fast if you venture too close.

Offer knowledge and seek their advice. Centaurs are well-traveled and value the knowledge gained from exploration; scholarly party members, like wizards and monks, may make an ally by offering a trade of information.

DON'T DO THIS

Don't mistake them for horses. Centaurs are not steeds for you to ride and will resent any remarks that insult their intelligence.

Don't pick a fight. Centaurs don't like to start fights, but they know how to finish them.

DISPLACER BEAST

SPECIAL POWERS

VERSATILE ASSAULTS
Their spiked tentacles hit like melee weapons and move independently, giving the displacer beast multiple options for attack.

DISPLACEMENT
Via magical illusion, the displacer beast appears to stand several feet away from its real location, making it difficult to both hit and avoid. If you do land a blow, this power is temporarily knocked out, giving you a better chance to win.

DARKVISION
Wicked, glowing eyes can pierce up to sixty feet (even through total darkness).

SIZE Displacer beasts are one-and-a-half times the size of a panther, the great cat they most resemble. With six legs, their bodies are long and lean.

Displacer beasts are vicious magical monsters that possess the otherworldly ability to displace light so that they appear to be several feet away from their actual location. This power makes them dangerous opponents, since it's hard to fight enemies who are never quite where they seem to be. They resemble sleek predatory cats covered in blue-black fur, with six legs and two spiked tentacles sprouting from their shoulders. Their eyes glow with a deep malice, a fire that cannot be dimmed even in death.

Originally bred by the Unseelie Fae (dark faeries) to hunt unicorns, pegasi, and other marvelous creatures, displacer beasts soon escaped and spread across the lands. They retain a love for the hunt, killing for sport as well as for food, and may toy with weaker prey before making a final strike. They hunt alone or in small packs, using their wicked intelligence to set up ambushes for unwary travelers. Don't let these dangerous creatures catch you by surprise!

LAIR Whether solo or in packs, displacer beasts favor densely wooded areas near roadways, where they can easily ambush prey. They can sometimes be found alongside intelligent evil creatures, such as vampire lords or mind flayers, serving as guards within their lairs.

DO THIS

Aim wide. Their displacement ability means these wicked beasts are never where they seem to be.

Be alert for tricks. Displacer beasts are cunning creatures, favoring strategy over straightforward assault.

DON'T DO THIS

Don't chase after a retreating displacer beast. It may be trying to lure you toward the rest of its pack!

Don't stick to a schedule. Displacer beasts are clever enough to remember the schedules of travelers passing by on a regular basis, so avoid an ambush by changing up when and how you travel.

OWLBEAR

SPECIAL POWERS

KEEN SIGHT AND SMELL
Owlbears have exceptionally good vision, even in the dark, and are skilled at sniffing out prey. You'll need to be extra-stealthy to avoid detection.

DEADLY FEROCITY
Stubborn and ferocious, nothing frightens away an owlbear. They will keep fighting long after a more sensible creature would have run away.

MULTIATTACK
These dangerous creatures can attack twice in the time it takes most monsters to strike once, biting with their sharp beaks and slashing with their deadly claws all at the same time.

SIZE Owlbears are slightly larger than a grizzly bear, weighing more than 500 pounds, and standing about three and a half feet tall when on all fours. They are almost seven feet long and tower over humans and even elves when standing on their hind legs.

Part giant owl, part enormous bear, these vicious creatures are densely muscled and covered in thick feathers. Their owl-like faces feature large, piercing eyes and a sharp beak, ready to tear apart the soft flesh of its prey. No one knows if these strange beasts were created by nature or by magic, but everyone knows to steer clear when they're on the prowl.

Emerging at night, owlbears hunt alone or in mated pairs, scouring around their lair for fresh food. They are intelligent enough to know their hunting grounds, using their awful screeches and hoots to drive prey into areas from which there is no escape.

Owlbears are difficult to control, although with enough food, time, and luck, they can be trained to perform basic tasks. Goblins sometimes employ them as war mounts, while hill and frost giants favor them as pets. Even tamed, these creatures are unpredictable and dangerous, quick to turn on their masters if food runs low.

LAIR Owlbears make their dens in caves or ruins littered with the bones of their prey. These foul lairs give off the stench of blood and death, attracting other predators to the area. Their nocturnal hunting patterns mean their dens may be left empty during the darkest hours of the night.

DO THIS

Use bait to distract their attacks. Creatures this big need a lot of food to feel full. If your party wants to avoid a fight, try distracting the owlbear with fresh meat placed nearby.

Watch out for other enemies. While many owlbears are solitary beasts, others may have a mate—or even some cubs—nearby. The loud screeching of an owlbear in battle is sure to draw the interest of other predators in the area.

DON'T DO THIS

Don't think you can scare them away. Owlbears are intelligent, but not smart enough to know when they're in a losing battle. Spellcaster illusions, no matter how impressive, won't be enough to stop this fight once it begins.

Don't poke around an empty lair for too long. These nocturnal predators know their hunting grounds well. Their keen sight and smell will inform them of an intrusion to their den even from miles away.

SPRITE

POISONS AND POTIONS

Sprites are experts at turning plants and flowers into poisons or potions that can hurt, burn, or sometimes heal. Their favorite elixir is a sleeping drink that they dab onto their arrows. The arrows are tiny, but the potion is strong enough to take down a full-size adventurer.

SIZE Sprites grow to just over a foot tall, which makes them slightly taller than an average full-grown house cat. (And they're often just as needy!)

When imagining the tiny, winged woodland creatures known as sprites, you might picture adorable flower fairies from children's picture books—but don't be fooled. Sprites are warriors, through and through.

Despite their small size, sprites are a tough and serious-minded race of fighters who protect the woods and forests from trespassers. They're excellent judges of character, and if you enter their land with bad intentions they will not hesitate to take you down. On the other hand, if you come seeking their aid for a righteous cause, you may just get it.

Sprites are not a lot of fun to be around, unless you're really into fighting. They don't value art or creativity at all, unless it's the art of war and creating new types of poison to put on the tips of their arrows. (They *really* love poison arrows.)

Sprites are experts at camouflage, and can sneak through the underbrush without being heard. If they really want to stay hidden, sprites can also turn invisible, but that only lasts until they attack.

LAIR Sprite villages look like human villages, except smaller. They may be built into tree branches or roots, or under a canopy of vines, with mushroom roofs and bamboo walls. Sprite villages are defended vigilantly by patrols.

DO THIS

Tread carefully through the forest. If you accidentally squash a sprite, their vengeance is merciless.

Have magical healing at the ready. If your party doesn't have a cleric, paladin, or druid to provide healing spells, then stock up on anti-poison potions before you enter sprite territory.

DON'T DO THIS

Don't go looking for their villages. They'll see you before you see them.

Don't think small means weak. Sprites may be tiny, but every inch is packed with fighting spirit.

TREANT

SPECIAL POWERS

A treant is never alone in a forest. If you ever go up against one treant, you'll discover that they can temporarily bring two other trees to life to work or fight alongside them. You might find yourself surrounded, without even knowing which trees you're fighting!

LAIR Treants live deep in wild forests, where they blend perfectly into their surroundings. Like ordinary trees, they live on sun, soil, and water, and they do not have any special or magical needs. Because treants are born from magic, their surroundings are often enchanted, and other magical beings may make their homes nearby.

SIZE Treants can grow as large as any tree. That means there could be a treant up to three hundred feet tall! Because they take so long to awaken, you're unlikely to find a small treant. Even a modestly sized one will be at least twice the height of a logging truck, so you know who'd win in that face-off!

If a tree ever falls in the forest, there are always other trees to hear it. And some may even mourn it.

Very old trees growing in sacred or magical spaces can sometimes gain a spark of consciousness. They contemplate their place in the world for a very long time, and when the time is right, they awaken . . . and move.

These awakened trees are called treants, and they are large and mighty beings. As they slowly come to life, treants develop humanoid features, including legs and arms created from their roots and branches, and wizened faces of bark and knots in their trunks. In their early years, they are often protected by older treants or by other guardians of the forest.

Upon maturity, they become protectors of the forest, sensitive to everything that happens around them. They use their great strength to defend the magic and wonder of nature—and to punish any who transgress. Few things can hit as hard as a fist of hardened oak!

Though treants can stand and move, they rarely travel far. They prefer a peaceful life of contemplation, enjoying the tranquility of nature while reflecting on the mysteries of existence.

DO THIS	DON'T DO THIS
Let druids and rangers take the lead. These nature-loving classes are the best equipped to approach a treant without giving it offense.	**Don't disrespect the forest.** Hurting healthy trees is the fastest way to anger a treant.
Regard every tree as if it could be a treant. When a treant is at rest, it looks exactly like other trees.	**Don't get lost in enemy territory.** Trying to hide from treants in trees is never a good idea.
Keep your fire-starter handy! If you ever have to keep an angry treant at bay, the threat of fire is very effective.	**Don't start forest fires.** Threats may hold them back, but a treant will move to attack if they see real flames within their woods.

UNICORN

☠
1

SPECIAL POWERS

Unicorns have several magical abilities, including the power to generate a protective field of shimmering energy, the ability to teleport up to a mile, and the power to heal the sick with the touch of its horn. Unicorns can also attack with their horns or their hooves, delivering magical damage.

SIZE Unicorns come in the same range of heights and sizes as ordinary horses. The unicorn's horn is the same length as an adult human forearm. These horns are known for their ability to channel magic. They can be ground up in potions or wielded like a wand. Forces of good will seek to punish anyone who uses a unicorn's horn in this way.

Unicorns look like horses with individual spiraling ivory horns, but they are actually something much stranger—celestial avatars of goodness that have come to the physical world from ethereal planes to protect sacred woodland spaces. Unicorns live in magic-rich forests, where they defend the innocent and vulnerable and try to keep the forces of evil at bay.

Attuned to nature, unicorns sense every sound and movement in the trees and bushes around them. They are also highly sensitive to virtue and can sense how good or bad a person is. They will gladly punish the unworthy (perhaps by skewering them with their horn), but they may also come to the aid of the worthy (usually by healing them of sickness or injury).

The most virtuous may even be allowed to ride a unicorn into battle against forces of great darkness, but this is very rare.

LAIR There are few places more beautiful than a unicorn's lair. Unicorns are so magical that their homes change to reflect their nature, resulting in peaceful glades and picture-perfect woodland scenes. In a unicorn's domain, birds sing more clearly and flowers seem to glow.

Other magical creatures are drawn to this sanctuary, where they are welcome under the unicorn's protection so long as they conduct themselves with virtue.

DO THIS

Approach with caution. If unicorns judge you unworthy to be in their presence, they'll let you know in a hurry.

Respect the unicorn's domain. Even a lifetime of good deeds won't help you if you try to steal magic from a unicorn.

DON'T DO THIS

Don't bring your hatred, jealousy, or evil into their domain. Unicorns will not tolerate any but the pure of heart within their sanctuary.

Don't seek power by using a unicorn's horn. They may be magical items, but they're not strong enough to protect you from the celestial forces that will seek revenge for your desecration.

UNICORN

As Kalista ventured deep into the forest, she could hear the fairy folk whispering and giggling. What could a creature like her ever want in a place like this? She flinched at every movement in the trees, yet she kept herself centered and calm. She had come to find an answer to a question, and she would not be turned away.

At last, she came to the clearing, a shallow pool of crystal-clear water nestled beneath silvery trees bursting with colorful blossoms, where she saw what she had come for. A unicorn drank from the pool, its magical horn seeming to shimmer in the midday light.

Kalista lived her whole life believing she was a monster. Born with obvious marks of her infernal tiefling heritage in a village that had never seen anything like her, she was told she carried darkness inside her and that her gifts of magic came from somewhere evil. The people she loved said that she was wicked and chased her from her home.

Yet she did not feel wicked in her heart.

Kalista was told unicorns could sense darkness in a person and would chase evil away from their sacred groves. She came to the forest to discover what the unicorn saw in her.

As she knelt near the noble creature, it looked up at her only briefly, and then returned its attention to the waters. The unicorn was not disturbed by her. It was not afraid. It was not threatened.

A tear ran down Kalista's cheek, for now she knew her heart had not lied.

Many would not have the courage to test themselves in such a way. If you ventured into an enchanted forest, how would the unicorn greet you?

GIANTS

Long before the empires of man, there were other kingdoms across these lands—the empires of the giants! These proud, titanic people were almost unopposed in their dominance of the world—except by the dragons, who would become their enduring foes.

Tales are still told of the epic wars between giants and dragons, which helped push both empires into decline. Today, giants live in remote and scattered clans, divided into six major races: hill giants, stone giants, frost giants, fire giants, cloud giants, and storm giants. All the races of giants have their own ideas about social standing that they call the *ordning*, which means "order." Storm giants look down on cloud giants, who look down on fire giants, who look down on frost giants, who look down on stone giants, who look down on hill giants. Hill giants aren't smart enough to know they're at the bottom, or smart enough to care. Each race also has their own way of figuring out rank within their own society, such as by wealth, strength, or even artistic talent. In hill giant society, your height and the size of your belly determine your social rank. They think bigger is always better!

Giants still cling to dreams of glory, and retain the physical strength and power to crush unwary travelers who cross their paths. If you ever happen across a giant, just hope that you're small enough to pass by unnoticed. That is, unless you think you're tough enough to take down a giant....

HILL GIANT

2

SIZE Even an average-size hill giant is taller than the largest African elephant—and probably a lot heavier too.

Of all the races of giants, hill giants are the ones you're most likely to run into on a very bad day. Heavy, dirty, stinky, and *mean*, they wander hills and valleys, plundering farms and homesteads for something to eat. Feeding their incredible appetites is really the only thing they care about, and you don't want to find yourself on the menu.

Hill giants look a lot like humans, but bigger and uglier, with a smell your nose might pick up from half a mile away. You'll likely find them dressed in ragged skins speckled with mud and brandishing a jagged old tree stump as a club. If you do see one, run away, because their attitude is just as nasty as their stench.

Nursery rhymes tell us that giants want to grind your bones to make their bread, but baking is probably a bit beyond a hill giant's skills, and it's definitely beyond their needs. They're more likely to eat you raw, in a few quick bites. They'll eat just about anything they can swallow, and they can swallow … just about anything.

LAIR Hill giants live in mud huts or simple wooden shacks on hillsides and in valleys. Sometimes they try to take over the settlements of other races that they've chased away or devoured, but they're so big that they tend to accidentally destroy the buildings instead.

DO THIS

Sniff the air. If there's a hill giant nearby, you might smell them before you see them.

Try to trick or hide from them. Because they're not very smart, hill giants are easy to deceive.

DON'T DO THIS

Don't try to reason with a hill giant. They're very bad at conversation.

Don't mistake any other type of giant for a hill giant. They will take great offence at the comparison.

Don't be too delicious!

STONE GIANT

READING THE RUNES Stone giants have developed a complex set of symbols they use to communicate stories and enchant magical items. They have great skill at carving rock and believe that studying carvings and runes can reveal the mysteries of the world. Prophecies are very popular among stone giants, and they might be persuaded to share some of their visions of the future with a thoughtful enough guest.

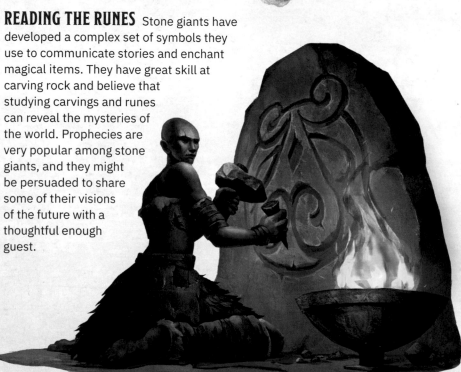

LAIR Stone giants love the dark and cold of the world far below our feet. Their elaborate networks of caves extend for miles. You can often identify these caves by the beautiful carved markings on the walls. Stone giants may live in communities, but they value peace and quiet so much that many also prefer to live alone.

SIZE At an average height of eighteen feet, stone giants are about as tall as one of those dancing tube figures that you might see outside a car dealership (though a stone giant probably wouldn't be very impressed if they met one).

Though stone giants rank just above hill giants (see page 40) in the social order, they are more civilized than their unruly cousins. They're not driven entirely by physical hunger, leaving them time to appreciate more complex concerns such as craft, contemplation, and solitude. Stone giants enjoy peace and quiet so much that the darker and quieter a place is, the more sacred they believe it to be. They're perfectly happy staying underground.

Because they live their lives almost entirely in caverns deep beneath the ground, stone giants have skin untouched by the sun and are almost as gray as the rocks that surround them. Get them above ground, however, and stone giants can be very dangerous. They regard the surface as a sort of dream world where nothing is real, and where their actions don't have consequences. The farther they are from home, the more trouble they can cause.

Stone giant society is ranked according to refinement and skill, whether it's the excellence of their artistry or their grace as athletes. Those who lack such talents are often relegated to the fringes of their community, serving as guards and hunters for their more sophisticated cousins.

DO THIS

Watch the walls. Stone giants can camouflage themselves against rock and stone.

Admire their work. Stone giants work hard on their craft, and they may respond well to flattery.

Meet them underground. The closer a stone giant is to the surface, the more violent they're likely to be.

DON'T DO THIS

Don't run. A stone giant can throw rocks far and with tremendous accuracy. If you're not careful, you could get squished before you reach safety.

Don't lose your way. If you venture into the caverns and cross paths with a stone giant, you'll want to remember the quickest way back to the surface.

FROST GIANT

TROPHIES Because frost giants love war, they also love trophies, whether taken from the settlements they've destroyed or made from the bodies of the enemies they've slain. That might include a majestic weapon or a jewel so huge that only a giant can wear it. But there's nothing a frost giant loves more than a trophy that shows they've bested a dragon.

If you're crossing the frozen wastelands and hear the wail of a war horn through the swirl of the frigid winds, it's probably already too late for you to run and seek shelter. The frost giants are coming.

Frost giants are weather-hardened warriors who make their homes in lands of ice and snow, where very little grows and even less survives. Their skin is blue and cold to the touch, and their hair is white and crusted with ice. They avoid the sun and shun fire. There is no room for warmth in a frost giant's life.

Because they live in such barren territory, frost giants raid and pillage for food and goods. As a result, their entire society is built around war and strength. In fact, the social order among frost giants is based on how tough you are, whether it's the size of your muscles or the number of scars you have. Frost giants are more than happy to test their strength against each other to see who comes out on top.

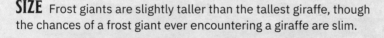

LAIR Frost giants reside in cold and desolate places, in ice-rimed glacial caves or on the highest snow-capped mountains. You're much more likely to encounter a frost giant on one of their raids into neighboring territory, but if you do ever stumble upon a frost giant's lair, don't expect a warm welcome.

SIZE Frost giants are slightly taller than the tallest giraffe, though the chances of a frost giant ever encountering a giraffe are slim.

DO THIS	DON'T DO THIS
Stay in the sun. Frost giants don't venture too far from home, and you'll never come across them in a warm climate.	**Don't show any weakness.** Frost giants only respect strength.
Listen for the war horn. If you're ever in territory that's close to a frost giant's lair, have your escape route planned in case you hear their war horn blare.	**Don't go into frozen wastelands.** At least not without a good dog pack or trusty steed to carry you swiftly out again.

FROST GIANT

Bruenor clung to the protected side of a snowy outcropping as his keen eyes scanned the mountain for movement. Wind whipped swirls of snow into the air, making it hard to judge distance or see imminent threats. After decades traversing the north, enduring some of the harshest weather imaginable in all of Faerûn, the dwarven warrior was used to the cold, but it didn't make his job any easier.

Just as Bruenor's mind started to wander with thoughts of cracking open his rations to have a snack, he saw his target: a frost giant, towering above the trees, marching along the mountain as easily as a human or dwarf would traverse a hiking trail. From Bruenor's hidden vantage point, the giant's head was almost level. He could see that its battered helmet and ring-mail armor spoke of many battles fought and won. Slung on its back was a double-headed axe large enough to chop a house in half.

The dwarf had an axe of his own, notched by dozens of brutal battles. The weapon had served him well over the years. If Bruenor charged now and jumped, he might be able to surprise the giant and wound it, giving him the advantage in combat. If he stayed hidden, he'd be safe, but then the giant would almost certainly attack the nearby village, once it saw smoke from the fires down below. Could the dwarf sneak away and warn them without being seen? Should he make a lot of noise and distract the giant instead?

Whatever he was going to do, he had to decide *now*.

What happens next? Does Bruenor attack the frost giant, using his mighty axe against his opponent—and if he does, is the weapon sharp enough to pierce the giant's thick hide? Does he remain hidden, thinking up a plan that will use his wits as well as his weapon to save the village? It's up to you!

FIRE GIANT

MASTERS OF THE FORGE

Fire giants are talented blacksmiths who excel at making armor, iron fortifications, and the deadliest and heaviest weapons, some of which are huge even by a giant's standards. However, as beautiful and well-crafted as their weapons can be, fire giants also share all giants' fondness for just hurling really big rocks.

SIZE Fire giants grow to an average height of about eighteen feet, which means they're about the right height to look through the upper window of a two-story house (if this happens to you, run for the fire escape)!

With skin as dark as ash and hair as bright as flame, everything about the fire giant reminds you of their obsession with fire. Their ornate armor and terrifying weapons should give you a clue about their other obsession: war.

Fire giants live in a militaristic society that prizes valor, conquest, and battle tactics. Fire giants train as soldiers their entire lives, and their social order is determined by both strength and intelligence (because winning a war is never *just* about might). Fire giants are highly competitive and many of their leaders are determined to advance their rank in the great ordning.

Blacksmiths are also held in high regard in fire giant society, as the blacksmith's forge is the heart of the fire giant war machine. Fire giants appreciate craft and skill, and their blacksmiths always work to improve their weapons and invent new ones to meet any challenge.

LAIR If you've ever wanted to visit a lair built inside a volcano, venture forth in search of the fire giants. They build incredible fortress castles underground, ideally on top of bubbling molten lava pits. If there isn't a volcano nearby, expect to find them mining for coal or destroying forests to fuel their enormous forges.

DO THIS	DON'T DO THIS
Stay cool. Fire giants don't like to venture far from a heat source.	**Don't underestimate them.** Fire giants value strength, but also intelligence. They're not simple brutes like hill giants.
Learn a song. Fire giants love war songs, so you might win their favor by appealing to their vanity and singing about their great victories. This is where your party's bard can really shine.	**Don't get caught.** Fire giants put their prisoners to work in the mines. So if they capture you, you might never escape.

DUKE ZALTO

💀
5

Like all fire giants, an average person would stand somewhere between Zalto's knee and his belt as he towers overhead. His arm is thicker than your whole body and each of his fingers are wider than your whole head.

Duke Zalto is a fire giant warlord with an obsession. Zalto believes he can become ruler of all giants by building an ancient war colossus called the Vonindod. An angry eighteen-foot-tall warrior with an even more gigantic monster machine? Yeah, it's a scary possibility and someone needs to stop him.

Even without the Vonindod, Zalto is tougher than the average fire giant. He's an experienced soldier who has fought in dozens of battles. He carries a massive *maul* (a war hammer wielded with two hands) that's so big he can keep a human-size prisoner in the cage on top, and he has two huge dogs (named Narthor and Zerebor) that follow him wherever he goes.

LAIR Zalto lives in Ironslag, a gargantuan stronghold embedded in Mount Hamarhaast, north of the Silver Marches. Standing at five hundred feet high, Ironslag is a multilevel fortress with twisting mines, a forge, and a prison. Entering Ironslag requires figuring out how to get past fifty-foot-tall adamantine doors sealed with ancient magic. Even if you do make your way inside, you'll have to contend with goblins, ogres, chimera, and the many fire giants loyal to the Duke before confronting Zalto himself.

ZALTO'S FAMILY Zalto is dangerous, and he's not alone. While exploring Ironslag, you may meet members of his family as well.

Brimskarda: Zalto's wife, an angry fire giant woman annoyed with her husband's desire to build the Vonindod.

Cinderhild: Zalto's daughter, a frustrated fire giant teen who wishes she could leave Ironslag and explore the world outside.

Zaltember: Zalto's son, a lazy and cruel fire giant teen who enjoys hurting smaller creatures for fun.

THE VONINDOD The Vonindod, also known as the Titan of Death, is an ancient construct that Zalto hopes to rebuild in order to raise his ranking within the giants' ordning.

If completed, the colossus will stand eighty feet tall with eyes made from giant rubies and armor of invulnerable adamantine. Four times the size of a fire giant, the Vonindod could wrestle an ancient dragon to the ground or punch a hole in a mountain with its huge metal hands. Zalto must be stopped before he brings the Vonindod back to life!

CLOUD GIANT

3

SPECIAL POWERS Cloud giants often use magic to control the weather—
to summon clouds or fog, to carry themselves on the wind or move objects
around, or even to call down lightning to destroy a foe. All cloud giants share
the ability to transform themselves into foggy mist and to walk on clouds.

SIZE Cloud giants are the second-largest race of giants,
averaging about twenty-four feet tall. That means
they're about the height of four tall men standing on
each other's shoulders.

If you've ever dreamed of climbing a beanstalk all the way up to the clouds and then venturing into a giant's home to steal their great treasures, the cloud giants would like to have a word with you. Because those are *their* treasures, and they don't want to share.

Pale, athletic, and distinguished, cloud giants live in a society defined by wealth and beauty. They dress in finery, adorn themselves with exotic jewels, and surround themselves with lavish treasures and wonderful works of art. Rank in cloud giant society is determined by wealth and by the beauty and generosity of one's gifts.

An elite race, cloud giants consider the world below to be a trivial place, only valuable as a source of more treasure or entertainment. They sometimes place bets on the outcomes of mortal wars. (Indeed, one of the only times they might interfere in the affairs of lesser races is when the wager isn't going their way.)

LAIR Cloud giants take pride in the beauty of their homes, so they would prefer that you *not* refer to them as "lairs." They live in palaces and castles, either high on mountaintops or up in the clouds themselves, which are surrounded by extravagant gardens of giant-size fruits and bright blooming flowers.

DO THIS

Show respect. Cloud giants can be very vain, and they appreciate flattery.

Watch out for their pets! Instead of keeping cats or dogs as pets, cloud giants keep griffons, giant eagles, or flying tigers.

Challenge them to a game. Cloud giants can't resist a challenge. If a cloud giant has you cornered, a game of chance may be your **only** hope of escape.

DON'T DO THIS

Don't steal. Proud of their homes and their treasures, cloud giants **won't** forget if you take something from them.

Don't hide. Cloud giants can sniff you out wherever you hide.

Definitely don't hide in the mist. Sometimes the mist **is** the cloud giant.

STORM GIANT

SPECIAL POWERS Just as the name suggests, storm giants are masters of the storm. Their innate magical abilities not only allow them to control weather (like their cloud giant cousins on page 52), but also to hurl lightning bolts directly from their hands. Storm giants also have the gift of prophecy. By reading patterns and omens, they can foretell the rise and fall of empires.

LAIR Storm giant lairs have one thing in common: they are almost impossible to reach. Whether storm giants choose to make their home on a remote mountain, in the deepest and darkest trench of an ocean, or so high up in the clouds that they can almost touch the stars, storm giants keep their distance. They don't even spend much time around each other and don't expect many visitors.

SIZE Storm giants are the biggest of all the giant races, and they grow to an average height of about twenty-six feet. That makes them about ten feet taller than a famous London double-decker bus.

Pale and elegant, storm giants are largely peaceful beings despite their terrifying size and tremendous power. They live for hundreds of years and have long memories, so most are happy watching history go by, waiting for the day when their kingdom grows strong again and they can rule the world once more.

Storm giants are typically distant and aloof. When they do sometimes bother to involve themselves in the affairs of smaller, more short-lived creatures though, they can bring an entire country to its knees. As you've already probably figured out, it's usually better to leave storm giants alone.

Even still, if you're looking for some advice, a visit to a storm giant can be very rewarding. They can see the past and catch glimpses of possible futures. Come to them with proper respect and a good heart, and they may be willing to help you.

Storm giants are above all other giants in rank, and they do not care about the power struggles of the giants beneath them. Among their own kind they rarely battle for status, preferring to live secluded lives of contemplation if possible.

DO THIS	DON'T DO THIS
Keep your distance. You could comfortably go your whole life without ever meeting a storm giant.	**Don't impose on a storm giant.** They enjoy their own company, not yours!
Show proper respect. Storm giants are wise and ancient. They're used to being treated like gods. If you disrespect them, they may destroy you . . . **and** everyone around you.	**Don't try to trick them.** Very little escapes storm giants' notice, and they have no time for fools.

MOORS, BOGS & BONEYARDS

The dead do not always rest peacefully. Graveyards may be filled with evil energy and dark creatures who are ready to strike out in envy against the living.

Nor are graveyards always where you think. The churchyard dotted with stone markers is obvious, but an open field may be the resting place of ancient warriors felled in a great battle, or a dark cave may mark where an orc tribe once disposed of their dead.

Boneyards are not alone in harboring dark energies. Windswept moors and swampy bogs are steeped in solitude and despair, a perfect domain for the restless undead.

Regardless of where you find them, these places contain both deadly forces and hidden treasures for the adventurer brave enough to challenge their dangers. Are you ready to face what lives outside life itself?

TURNING THE UNDEAD

The undead are unholy creatures existing in a state no longer living but also not quite deceased. For this reason, holy power wielded by the faithful can force undead monsters to turn away, flee, or, in some extreme cases, even explode on the spot. Cleric or paladins of certain faiths have access to this turning power, and it can be quite a potent tool when battling creatures risen from the dead.

BANSHEE

☠ 2

SPECIAL POWERS

HORRIFYING VISAGE
By distorting their terrifying faces, the banshee can render their opponents immobile with fear!

DETECTION OF LIFE
Banshees are drawn to the energy of living creatures, whose presence can be sensed up to five miles away.

INCORPOREAL MOVEMENT
Banshees can move through objects and other creatures with mild difficulty. Doors and walls won't stop them!

WAIL
Once per night, a banshee can unleash a horrifying scream that causes physical damage to any living creature within range.

Across the darkness of the night, a terrible wail sounds, sending fear shivering down the spine of even the bravest warrior. It is the call of the banshee, the corrupted spirit of a female elf. These cursed creatures misused their great beauty in life and are now condemned to suffer for their cruelty in death.

Banshees feel no joy or happiness, only pain at the presence of living creatures who remind them of all they have lost. They hoard beautiful treasures, surrounding themselves with art, jewels, and other objects reflecting their vanity in life. They mourn for their own lost loveliness, and a single glance in a mirror will drive one into a murderous rage. Few are prepared to face a banshee's full wrath!

LAIR Banshees are bound to the place of their death and cannot travel more than five miles from that spot. Many died in once-luxurious mansions, now crumbling to dust, and others expired in the wilderness, having driven away everyone who cared for them in life.

SIZE As the spirit of a female elf, banshees retain roughly the same shape and size in death. Their forms are luminous and wispy, surrounded by a tangle of wild hair and tattered rags that float around them in a ghostly manner.

DO THIS

Fight from a distance. The banshee's touch carries a necrotic energy that does damage to living creatures.

Use magical weapons and attack spells. Banshees are resistant to all types of damage from normal weapons, so now's the time to break out that magic sword or fireball spell.

DON'T DO THIS

Don't show off your treasures. Banshees covet beautiful objects and will stop at nothing to add your shiny things to their collections.

Don't count on walls, gates, or other obstacles to protect you. A banshee can phase right through such objects to reach her target.

SKELETON

PAST LIVES Skeletons have no conscious memory of their past selves, but many retain habits from their former lives. These habits sometimes emerge when a skeleton is left without specific orders to follow. For instance, a skeleton of a farmer might start hoeing the ground, or the skeletons of nobles might carry out an eternal dance in an abandoned ballroom.

Lacking memory of language, skeletons cannot speak, so they communicate only with basic gestures.

SIZE A skeleton's size changes based on the bones used to create it. While standard races such as humans and elves are most common, powerful mages have managed to revive the bones of huge creatures, like dragons and giants—not to mention cobbling together unique creations from a mix of different bones!

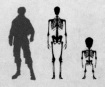

Animated by dark magic, skeletons are bony warriors summoned forth by spellcasters or who arise of their own accord from graves steeped in necromantic energy and ancient evils. In whatever fashion they are created, these relentless foes fight without mercy and attack until destroyed—for the evil energy that made them also drives them to kill all living creatures.

Obedient servants, skeletons are capable of complex tasks, like firing a catapult or dropping boiling oil on enemies below, provided each step is carefully explained. They move and fight in a simple manner, pursuing their goals with mindless determination, and make excellent guards.

While most skeletons are humanoid, bones of all types can be brought back to life with powerful enough magic, and adventurers may find themselves facing down all manner of strange and deadly skeletal forms!

LAIR Skeletons may be found in the graveyards or ancient battlegrounds where their bones once laid at rest. They can also be found guarding castles and estates for necromancers and other powerful sorcerers.

DO THIS

Fight like your life depends on it. Skeletons never give up, so you can't either!

Take advantage of obstacles. Skeletons' limited mental capacity means they are easily slowed by doors, furniture, and other hindrances.

Call upon your party's clerics. Divine magic allows clerics to turn the undead, the only power that can stop a skeleton's relentless attacks.

DON'T DO THIS

Don't try to reason with them. They won't be swayed, no matter how charismatic you are.

Don't underestimate how they'll attack. Most skeletons fight in a simple, straightforward manner, but they're capable of complex battle moves if orders are given carefully enough.

SKELETON

It was an easy gig. That's what the thieves' guild had promised Shandie when she took the assignment. Ride in, grab the goblet, ride back out.

Nobody mentioned the curse, or the skeletons that came with it.

Shandie had seen the green light when she lifted the goblet from its pedestal, and had felt the flow of some malevolent energy rattle across her fingertips before it dispersed into the night. There had been silence for a moment, broken only by the sound of wind through the spruce trees outside and the buzz of a persistent mosquito that'd been tailing her since her last river crossing. Then there came a dreadful grinding, like old bones being rubbed together, and the damp thump of moving dirt.

The halfling whirled around, unsheathing her trusty short sword. One skeleton she could handle, but she'd spotted a graveyard on her way in. Who knows how many of these things would be summoned by the curse? Shandie considered putting the goblet back where she'd found it, which might be enough to calm them down and disperse the evil magic that summoned them. Then again, the payout for this job was pretty sweet. Maybe she could fight her way through them all . . . if she was fast enough. She weighed the goblet in one hand and her sword in the other, trying to make a choice in the scant seconds left before the skeleton attacked.

What should Shandie do next? If she does defeat the skeleton in front of her, how many more will be waiting outside? If she puts the goblet back in its place, will that be enough to break the spell? Can she find a way to escape that uses her wits and speed more than her sword? It's up to you!

VAMPIRES

Vampires are the risen dead, hungering for the life they have lost—a yearning only satisfied by drinking the blood of the living! Undeath twists what few emotions vampires retain: love becomes sick obsession; friendship warps to bitter jealousy. They replace feelings with physical objects that stand in for lost emotions, collecting art and treasures that soothe—momentarily—their eternal emptiness.

Lands infested by one of these creatures see an increase in the numbers of vermin. Plants wither, or grow in twisted knots, while shadows move of their own accord and a creeping fog clings to the earth. Only slaying the vampire can lift the blight.

Vampire spawn are created when a vampire feeds on a living creature and allows its victim to expire without tasting the vampire's blood in return. The spawn gain some of the vampire's powers, including regeneration, which allows the monster to slowly restore its health during combat (unless it is unconscious), and spider climbing, which allows the creature to easily scale difficult surfaces, such as vertical walls and upside down on ceilings!

Although mighty, vampires and their spawn have their weaknesses. Sunlight burns them, and they cannot cross running water, such as a stream or river. Their curse prevents them from entering a home unless invited inside by a resident. Their forms cast neither shadows nor reflections, and many a mortal has been saved by noticing a missing reflection before the vampire's fangs find their throat. Finally, a wooden stake driven through their heart instantly paralyzes a vampire, leaving them vulnerable to death by decapitation.

VAMPIRE LORD

4

SPECIAL POWERS

CHARM
A living victim influenced by this power sees the vampire as a trusted friend, making them open to the creature's suggestions and willing to receive its bite!

SUMMONING
During the night, a vampire may call a horde of bats or rats to do their bidding; when outside, they can also command a pack of wolves in the same way!

SHAPESHIFTING
Vampires can transform into a bat, letting them fly while retaining all their mystical powers.

MIST
When injured, a vampire converts into a cloud of mist that flees toward its resting place. If a misted vampire reaches its coffin, it can regenerate its physical body!

SIZE Vampires are transformed humanoids and have the same size as a typical member of their mortal species.

Alone, a vampire is a formidable enemy. Clever and cunning, they may use charm to sway mortals to their service, or spy unseen in one of their shape-changing forms. They are fierce fighters, moving with alarming speed and delivering a deadly bite with their sharp fangs. Even when your weapons land solid blows, the vampire's ability to regenerate pulls victory further from your grasp!

But worse, these fearsome creatures surround themselves with loyal servants, both their own spawn and other undead, who protect their master at any cost. Vampires can exist forever, draining the blood of the living and infesting the surrounding lands with the aura of their evil presence. Their eternal scourge can only be ended by the courage and strength of a mighty adventurer!

LAIR Vampires choose majestic yet defendable lairs, often castles or manors. Their coffins are typically hidden in underground crypts or guarded vaults. They are forced to lie within their coffins during the day, but can move this location by transporting the coffin or a large amount of grave dirt to a new resting spot.

DO THIS

Call upon nature's power. Sunlight and running water are among the greatest weaknesses of a vampire, so find ways to bring those into your battle!

Bring along a holy spellcaster. If your party doesn't already have a cleric, now is a good time to ask the local churches if anyone is willing to join you on your quest. Their ability to turn the undead is crucial when fighting vampires.

DON'T DO THIS

Don't ignore the warning signs. If the locals are worried about an increase in rats or creepy mist that rolls in at sunset, a vampire may be taking up residence. Root it out before it can establish a formidable lair!

Don't forget to look up. A vampire's climbing powers mean it can attack from several directions, including overhead.

VAMPIRE SPAWN

3

SPECIAL POWERS As creatures weaker than their makers, vampire spawn do not possess the full range of undead powers. They can call upon only regeneration and spider climb (see page 65). Vampire spawn may also use their claws and teeth for dangerous attacks!

SIZE Vampire spawn are transformed humanoids and have the same size as a typical member of their mortal species. However, their physical size does not always reflect the cursed strength they possess!

Vampire spawn are ravenous creatures under the control of their creator, loyal and obedient to all commands. They share the vampire's endless thirst, and seek out fresh victims whenever their master allows. Their lack of free will means they cannot access the most powerful of the vampire's abilities, but their feral cunning and relentless hunger have still been the downfall of many adventurers.

Some vampires create spawn specifically to function as servants or guards, devoted during the night and hiding in their coffins during the day. Other spawn may be used to prey upon the living residents of the vampire's realm, spreading fear and death wherever they go. Either way, the eternal loyalty of vampire spawn can only be broken by the death of their creator—which gives them back their free will.

LAIR You'll find vampire spawn within the grand castles and mansions of their vampire master. A rare few may haunt lonely graveyards or other remote sites, chained to their burial place by their undead curse.

DO THIS

Stock up on stakes. The paralysis wears off once the stake is removed, so you'll need one for every vampire spawn you're up against.

Keep a mirror near your front door. That way, you can be sure any strangers seeking help in the night have a reflection before you let them in.

DON'T DO THIS

Don't negotiate. The bond between a vampire spawn and its master is mystical in nature and cannot be broken, even by threats of death.

Don't delay in dealing with them. Once their master is killed, vampire spawn regain their free will—which means they may come after you looking for revenge.

COUNT STRAHD VON ZAROVICH

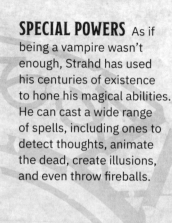

SPECIAL POWERS As if being a vampire wasn't enough, Strahd has used his centuries of existence to hone his magical abilities. He can cast a wide range of spells, including ones to detect thoughts, animate the dead, create illusions, and even throw fireballs.

In life, Count Strahd was a prince, a soldier, a conqueror, and a student of dark magics. Hundreds of years into his vampiric reign over Barovia, a vast valley filled with dark forests and surrounded by looming mountains, he is all this and more, a terrifying creature of remorseless evil and cold brilliance. Detached from all human emotion, Strahd takes joy in the conquest of mortal souls, corrupting where he can and destroying where he cannot. His vampire powers are enhanced by powerful spellcasting, including the ability to animate the dead!

The doors of Ravenloft Castle, Strahd's realm, are always unlocked; those who enter must prepare themselves to face a remorseless enemy who delights in testing his opponents with both brute force and treachery. Is your party up to the task?

LAIR Count Strahd dwells within the mighty castle of Ravenloft, an opulent gothic structure protected by hordes of undead creatures. His mystical connection with his lair allows him to pass through its walls without resistance or open and lock doors with just a thought. Strahd's evil influence has spread eternal night not only over the castle but across the entire land of Barovia—a darkness only you can dispel by defeating the count himself.

STRAHD'S MINIONS To really fight Strahd, you'll need to get through the dangerous creatures who guard him first. Within the halls of Ravenloft, you'll find wolves and bats, ghosts and ghouls, even skeletons and vampire spawn.

HEART OF SORROW Hidden deep within the walls of Ravenloft is a giant crystal called the Heart of Sorrow. Any damage that Count Strahd takes during combat is magically transferred to this gem, allowing him to shrug off the mightiest of blows. You'll need to find and destroy this magical crystal before you can take Count Strahd down for good!

SIZE In his normal form, Count Strahd is a tall, muscular humanoid, clad in expensive robes and armor. His shapeshifting powers allow him to transform into a small bat, a medium-size wolf, and an untouchable cloud of mist.

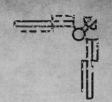

OCEANS, LAKES & WATERWAYS

Water is the source of life. We came from that primordial swirl, it sustains every growing thing around us, and we return to it all the time, to drink, to bathe, and to experience tranquility.

Don't be fooled. Water brings life, but it can also take it. There are plenty of creatures lurking beneath the waves that might wish you harm ... and many of them have teeth!

Out in the depths, something great and terrible may be swimming toward an unsuspecting fisherman. Closer to the shoreline, an unwary explorer may cross an unseen boundary, entering the territory of a fierce and merciless foe. Even in lakes and rivers, a charming stranger could lure you to your doom.

If you thought it was safe to drink from a stream or soak in the sea, think again. Deadly creatures may be lurking just beneath the surface.

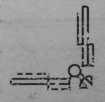

ABOLETH

SPECIAL POWERS An aboleth can strike you with its tail or tentacles or contaminate you with its mucus; but that's not even the worst. Their psychic attacks allow them to enslave your mind, controlling your actions and draining your energy to heal itself.

SIZE Aboleths usually grow to about twenty feet in length, which makes them about a third bigger than a female great white shark. However, there are reports that some of the most ancient and powerful aboleths can grow to twice that size.

With eyes as dark as the deepest ocean, mouths with more deadly teeth than any shark, and long, writhing, powerful tentacles that exude toxic mucus, you may imagine that aboleths are some of the most terrifying predators under the sea. They *are*, and even worse than you can envision!

These huge and terrible creatures are the fallen masters of lost civilizations, and their most potent weapons are their minds. Aboleths have the power to psychically enslave mortal creatures, and they once abused this power to make people worship them, forcing the compelled masses to build temples in their honor.

The true gods took offense at this sacrilege and destroyed the aboleths' empire. The aboleths have lurked in darkness ever since, vowing to one day have their revenge.

Aboleths never forget an enemy. In fact, aboleths never forget anything. Even worse, aboleths never truly die, so if you ever destroy one, it will eventually come back ... and then it will come for you.

LAIR Ruins of ancient aboleth civilizations still survive to this day, deep in the dark recesses of the ocean or in flooded caverns far beneath our feet. Proud and bitter aboleths still swim among these ruins, where their magic is at its strongest. Aboleths can control the foul water flowing through their lairs and use it to drown unwary visitors or as a channel for their psychic rage.

DO THIS	DON'T DO THIS
Stay in the shallows. Steer clear of deep water that contains ancient ruins or clouds of mucus.	**Don't believe your eyes.** Aboleths can get inside your head and cast illusions.
Guard your thoughts. Before you meet an aboleth, find a spell or artifact that can protect you against mind attacks.	**Don't trust anyone who tells you aboleths are okay.** They're probably being mind-controlled.

DRAGON TURTLE

SPECIAL POWERS

AMPHIBIOUS
Dragon turtles can breathe both air and water, allowing them to move swiftly between environments.

BASHING ATTACK
With a single smash of their mighty tails, dragon turtles can knock their opponents off their feet and push them ten feet away, making it impossible to fight back.

STEAM BREATH
Dragon turtles can shoot out a sixty-foot blast of boiling-hot steam that injures everyone in its path.

SIZE An adult dragon turtle is between thirty-five and sixty feet long and can weigh up to 250,000 pounds. That's about the size of an old-fashioned sailing ship, and the same weight as a space shuttle.

Dragon turtles are among the most fearsome of all ocean dwellers, capable of taking down ships with their crushing jaws, steaming breath, and smashing tails. Their enormous shells are a deep green color, the same shade as the ocean depths where they reside. Silver patterns on their shells mimic light bouncing off the waves, making them hard to spot by even the most diligent lookout.

Although not true dragons (see page 87), these creatures share their namesake's love of treasure. Clever sailors will bribe dragon turtles with jewels and other glittering goodies in exchange for safe passage through watery realms. Unlucky mariners will find their ship capsized by an attack, during which the dragon turtle swallows all the treasure it can find for transport back to its underwater cave.

LAIR Dragon turtles live in caves hidden among coral reefs, below the sea floor, or along a rugged coastline. Their lairs glitter with stolen treasure, and they tolerate no intruders.

DO THIS

Keep watch from the crow's nest. Dragon turtles may attack day or night. Watch for unnatural patterns of light on the water—that may mean a dragon turtle is close at hand.

Be ready to bribe them. Your party might decide that a shiny bauble is less valuable than safe passage through a dragon turtle's domain.

Find a crew who knows the dangers of the sea. Before you book passage, talk with the ship's crew to ensure they're prepared for the risks that might lie ahead.

DON'T DO THIS

Don't waste your arrows. A dragon turtle's thick shell is impenetrable to all but the mightiest of magics. If you must attack with non-magical weapons, aim for the softer underbelly.

Don't think that a life raft will save you. Abandoning ship won't be enough to save you from a dragon turtle, not if they think you've brought treasure with you on your escape.

MERROW

TOOTH AND CLAW The bite of a merrow can do a lot of damage, but the slash of its claws is even more dangerous. Here's the really bad news: a merrow will often attack with both teeth and claws at once.

SIZE Merrow grow to a length of about twelve feet, which is about as long as two terrified humans placed end to end as they desperately try to escape a merrow's grasp.

There are tribes of gentle merfolk living beneath the waves, peaceful communities that love to swim and play. The merrow are not those merfolk.

Legend says a tribe of merfolk fell under the curse of an ancient artifact that bound them to Demogorgon, a diabolical being also known as the Prince of Demons (see page 20). Ensnared by Demogorgon's madness, the merfolk's king conducted a ritual that opened a gateway to the Abyss, Demogorgon's dark dimension.

As a result, the merfolk were corrupted with madness and distorted into monstrous new forms, with sharklike teeth and terrible claws. They emerged from the Abyss as a new race of vicious predators who would attack ships, drown and devour sailors, and hoard treasures. They delight in spreading chaos and fear, which serves to feed the power of their demon lord.

LAIR If you ever find a string of corpses threaded together beneath the sea, beware; you are at the boundary of a merrow lair. This ghoulish display warns adventurers not to try their luck raiding the deep-sea caves of the merrow, which are often rich with plundered loot and sunken treasures.

DO THIS	DON'T DO THIS
Stay alert at the water's edge. Merrow can surge out of the sea in a flash.	**Don't stray into unknown waters alone.** You never know what dangers may lurk beneath, so be sure to bring backup.
Watch each other's backs in a merrow fight. Their skill at stealth means all members of your party need to protect one another or risk being hit with an unexpected attack.	**Don't play with strange artifacts.** If you don't know what something does, don't play with it—unless you want to wind up as cursed as the merrow.

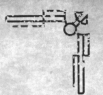

MOUNTAIN PEAKS & OPEN SKY

In the skies above us, monsters make their homes at the top of mountains, soaring through the air or floating just out of reach. These flying creatures can assault their targets from above or swoop down and strike when least expected. The sky is their playground and they know how to use it to their advantage.

A battle in flight can be more dangerous than almost any other. Not only can attacks come from any side at any time, but losing means falling from incredible heights to crash down upon the ground. The denizens who make the air their home can be vicious against those who wish to visit their domain. Are you ready to fly?

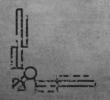

GRIFFON

RIDING A GRIFFON A fully grown wild griffon will never let you ride it and will likely tear you to pieces if you try.

However, if you find a griffon's egg and raise a griffon from a hatchling, you might be able to train it to be your loyal steed, and a griffon will serve you extremely well in battle. If you don't know *how* to train a griffon, it will probably tear you to pieces.

SIZE Though they have the body of a lion and the head and wings of an eagle, griffons are a little bigger than lions and a *lot* bigger than eagles. Even the most powerful stallion might be no match for a griffon's claws and beak.

A horse can be an adventurer's best friend when it comes to covering large distances in a short time and carrying plenty of weapons, supplies, or treasures with you. However, your best friend has its own worst enemy, as you'll discover if you ever ride your horse into griffon territory.

Griffons have the head, wings, and claws of an eagle, and the body and strength of a lion, all of which make them powerful and terrifying hunters. Their favorite prey? Horses. Griffons live in prides, like lions, and each pride is fiercely protective of its territory. Moving with the speed of an eagle, they can swoop down on you in a flash—and after they strike with the force of a lion, you may be finished off before you know what hit you. Of course, they're usually more interested in your horse than they are in you.

LAIR Griffons live on craggy mountains, where they build giant nests among the cracks and crevices. If you ever get a close look at a griffon's nest, you might notice that it's not just made of sticks and grass; it may also be made of the bones of their prey. Oh, and if you're that close to a griffon's nest, you're probably next on the menu.

DO THIS	DON'T DO THIS
Ride in disguise. Buy some camouflage for your horse before entering griffon territory to avoid attacks.	**Don't rush in at full gallop.** You hear clattering hooves, but a griffon hears the ringing of a dinner bell.
Jump off if a griffon grabs your horse. The beast will hold on to its prey and let you escape.	**Don't steal their eggs!** The idea of a raised-from-birth griffon mount sounds great now, but it won't be as much fun when mamma griffon comes after her baby.
	Don't mistake a griffon's cry for an eagle's. The griffon's cry is much deeper and louder—and getting it wrong could be deadly!

PEGASUS

1

RIDING A PEGASUS

Pegasi are as intelligent as many humanoid races, which means they can't be broken and tamed like ordinary horses. The only way you'll get to ride a pegasus is if they let you, which means building a bond of trust first. Pegasi have a strong sense of right and wrong, and they'll only trust you if they sense that you're a good person.

SIZE Pegasi come in the same variety of sizes as regular horses, but with one big difference— wings. Pegasus wings can extend to a span of about twenty feet, which is about the width of a townhouse!

The wild and wondrous pegasus is a rare sight for any adventurer to behold. While ordinary horses are an everyday encounter for many, you could live a hundred years and never see a single one of these winged wonders, both because pegasi are so uncommon and because they prefer to keep their distance from others.

According to legend, pegasi originate from another plane of reality, a realm of stunning beauty protected by elflike beings. The rulers of this realm ride the flying beasts as their steeds. Sometimes pegasi travel through into the ordinary world, perhaps to come to the aid of those who truly need their help.

Pegasi retain the wild nature and otherworldly majesty of their home realm. All pegasi are white as snow, but their wings and their coloration are not the only things that mark them apart from ordinary horses. They're also much smarter, which is why they keep their distance from the dangerous worlds of men and monsters.

LAIR Pegasi spend most of their time in the air, their wings never tiring. They typically only set down on the ground to eat or drink. When they do so, it's often in remote locations where there's no one else around.

DO THIS	DON'T DO THIS
Approach slowly and with respect. These clever creatures are quick to flee from those they do not trust.	**Don't try to tame a pegasus.** They will resist.
Treat pegasi as your equals. They're as smart as any human and will not tolerate being treated as simple beasts of the field.	**Don't try to sneak up on them.** They will fly away in a hurry.
	Don't feed them too many sugar cubes. Sugar is bad for their teeth—and for yours!

DRAGONS

In worlds of fantasy and adventure, stories are told about the most famous of magical creatures—*dragons!* Sometimes called wyrms, these are dangerous winged reptiles who covet treasure and slay any who cross their paths. They are spoken of in whispers by common townsfolk, and legends are told of those who battled them and lived. A young dragon can terrify a village, while an ancient wyrm can lay waste to an entire army.

Evil dragons are chromatic—white, green, black, blue, and red. Each has different abilities and breath weapons, and uses a different environment as a lair. If you seek a reputation as a slayer of dragons, understanding these differences might save your life.

The size and power of a dragon depends on its age, which also determines its danger level. Wyrmlings are baby dragons, younger than 5 years, who are as tall as a human and quite vulnerable. Young dragons are 6 to 100 years old and between eight and sixteen feet tall. An adult dragon is 101 to 800 years old and between sixteen and thirty-two feet tall. Ancient dragons are older than 800 years. These gargantuan terrors are more than thirty-two feet tall, and some can reach forty feet or larger.

All adult dragons can beat their wings so powerfully that they create gusts of wind to knock over targets. They also have powerful jaws that can rend flesh and bone, as well as incredibly sharp claws that are able to pierce non-magical armor with ease. Larger dragons can swing their tails like massive prehensile clubs, battering foes to the ground. And older dragons generate a supernatural fear that can terrify their opponents just by being near them.

WHITE DRAGON

☠ 3-5

SPECIAL POWERS

COLD BREATH
These cold-hearted dragons can exhale a terrifying icy blast that can tear a target apart with chunks of ice or freeze them solid.

ICE WALK
White dragons can walk across ice and snow without slipping or getting stuck.

White dragons might be the smallest, least intelligent, and most primitive of the evil chromatic dragon types, but don't let that fool you into thinking they're easy to defeat. Driven by hunger and greed, they are viciously cruel reptiles who live in cold climates.

These pale dragons may not have the same level of tactics and cunning as their more intelligent cousins, but their animalistic nature makes them skilled hunters. Once they decide on a target, white dragons stay incredibly focused on their prey, letting nothing get in the way of the kill.

LAIR White dragons live in icy caves and deep subterranean chambers far from the light of the sun. They love vertical heights in their caverns and will sometimes fly up and latch on to the ceiling like huge bats. Older white dragons naturally give off magic that lowers the temperature around them, leeching heat from the surrounding area.

White dragons eat only frozen food. They use their devastating ice-breath attack to flash-freeze victims, then store their prey inside their icy lairs to serve as snacks when they're hungry.

DO THIS

Stay warm. White dragons will try to slow you down by chilling you to the bone or freezing you solid. Make sure to dress warmly when hunting these frosty foes.

Watch your step! With ice and snow everywhere in a white dragon's lair, it's easy to slip and lose your footing.

DON'T DO THIS

Don't tell them your name. White dragons are the most vengeful of all chromatic dragons. They never forget a face and can carry a grudge for as long as they live. If you tick off a white dragon, it'll come after you looking for revenge!

Don't underestimate them. They may be less intelligent than other chromatic dragons, but they're still incredibly dangerous!

GREEN DRAGON

3-5

SPECIAL POWERS

POISON BREATH
These stinky dragons can exhale a grotesque cloud of green gas that makes creatures ill and causes them to choke as they gasp for air.

AMPHIBIOUS
Green dragons can breathe underwater, and some of them hunt by springing up from hiding places beneath the surface of lakes or large ponds.

Green dragons are the most cunning and treacherous of all the evil chromatic dragons. They're nasty tempered and aggressive, eager to take territory and show off their power. They have long necks and legs, so they easily step over underbrush in forests and poke their heads up through the trees while keeping all four feet on the ground.

Intelligent and cruel, green dragons enjoy hunting and proving their superiority. If a target is weak, they'll happily torment their prey, holding off on the final kill until they've had their fun. Green dragons will eat any creature they kill, but their absolute favorite meal is elves, fresh and choking on poison from the dragon's toxic-breath attack.

LAIR Green dragons lurk in old forests and, over time, their presence will bring a disgusting-smelling fog to the area. They look for caves to turn into lairs, and some even dig out their own and then cover the entrance with thick vegetation.

DO THIS

Use your nose. Look out for smelly fog when traveling in a forest. It's a clear sign that a green dragon may be lurking nearby.

Watch out from all directions. Green dragons can attack from the air above the tree line or by quickly slipping through the forest to strike. They're built to use the trees to their advantage.

DON'T DO THIS

Don't get poisoned. As soon as you see a green dragon start to inhale, cover your face with a cloak or other material and try to get out of the way of its poison breath. The choking, stinging fog will obscure your sight and leave you open to attack!

Don't underestimate them! If a green dragon thinks it's going to lose a fight, it will quickly surrender and may even act helpful, but it's just looking for an opportunity to regain its advantage and destroy the heroes that brought it low.

GREEN DRAGON

Krydle pressed himself against the moss-covered tree and tried to stay still. If he moved, Goreedus the dragon would know he was there.

Goreedus craned his long, scaled neck around the twisted branches, looking through the marshy forest for any sign of disturbance. The dragon's piercing emerald eyes could see insects flitting in the stagnant air and tadpoles swimming perfect little circles in the water, but nothing else. No sign of the cloaked thief it detected mere moments ago.

"Human... I know you are hiding... hoping I will leave you to carry on your pitiful life."

Krydle disagreed with the "pitiful" descriptor, but the rest was accurate.

"In a few moments, I will breathe a cloud of poison that will make you choke and vomit, revealing your location. Then I will grab you with a clawed hand and rend you limb from limb."

That sounded quite unpleasant. Krydle's nose furrowed.

"If you step forth now and show yourself, I will ask you three questions and then grant you mercy. If you stay hidden, there is only death."

Krydle had seconds to decide: Reveal himself and hope for the best, or quietly take a deep breath and try not to ingest in any of the toxic fumes about to fill the air all around him?

What should Krydle do? If he steps forward, does the dragon instantly attack or does it give him a chance to negotiate? What could Krydle even say to keep a dragon from eating him? On the other hand, if Krydle holds his breath, what happens when the dragon's poison cloud lasts longer than he can manage without air? It's up to you!

BLACK DRAGON

3-5

SPECIAL POWERS

ACID BREATH
These dragons can exhale a spray of burning acid, scorching anyone unlucky enough to be hit by it.

AMPHIBIOUS
Black dragons can breathe underwater, and some hunt by lying in wait beneath fetid and murky waters in large swamps.

Black dragons are the most sadistic of all the evil chromatic dragons. They enjoy destruction, and revel in turning vibrant places into rotting holes of decay.

Black dragons hate weakness and gleefully slay their most vulnerable enemies first, ensuring a quick and brutal victory. They cannot stand to be defeated or dominated, and would rather die than call someone else their "master."

LAIR You can find black dragons in rotting swamps or crumbling ruins, places that perfectly reflect their own destructive desires. Carrion eaters and insects tend to gather where black dragons live, cleaning the bones of the dragons' many rotting victims.

Over time, the land near a black dragon's lair will grow thick with twisted plants and reeking mud. Any sources of water near the dragon's lair will become corrupted and undrinkable, stained by the wyrm's foul presence.

DO THIS

Watch for ruins! Black dragons use ruins and swamps as their homes, so pay attention when exploring ancient places or marshlands.

Protect your group. Black dragons will focus on adventurers who aren't wearing armor, looking to exploit weakness. Make sure healers and magic-users are well protected, and keep armored combatants up front.

DON'T DO THIS

Don't get burned! Protect exposed flesh from nasty acid burns. Wear a heavy cloak and be prepared to cover yourself if the creature unleashes its powerful breath attack.

Don't underestimate them. Black dragons would rather die than surrender. In the final stages of a battle, a black dragon may lash out with desperation, so be careful!

BLUE DRAGON

3-5

SPECIAL POWERS

LIGHTNING BREATH
Blue dragons can exhale bolts of
lightning that scorch and blind foes.

SAND CLOUDS
Older blue dragons can summon
clouds of stinging sand to blind
and confuse their enemies.

Blue dragons are the most patient and methodical of all the evil chromatic dragons. They build their lairs patiently and hunt prey slowly and tactfully. A blue dragon knows that time is on its side, and its power will overtake almost any foe in the long run.

These dragons are the most likely to hire evil minions to help enact their schemes. They may covet gemstones and jewelry, but they know the value of a good servant too, and are willing to sacrifice from their treasure hoard to reward loyal service.

LAIR Blue dragons tend to live in desolate areas—badlands, broken steppes, and deserts. They build elaborate caves of crystal by using their lightning breath to fuse sand into shimmering caverns beneath the earth.

Thunder and lightning tend to gather near the lairs of older blue dragons, as do sand storms and tornados. The loud wind and booming air make for perfect cover when a blue dragon attacks unwary visitors.

DO THIS

Check the weather. Storm clouds or whipping winds in a desert may be signs that a blue dragon lives nearby.

Close the gap. Blue dragons have an advantage if they avoid close combat, so they keep their distance and pummel enemies with powerful bolts of lightning. Move in as soon as you can and don't let them escape!

DON'T DO THIS

Don't show your bling. Blue dragons collect gemstones—the larger and more valuable, the better. If they see you have pretty gemstones, they might just make you their next target.

Don't lose your temper. Blue dragons are patient and methodical in both schemes and battles. They expect their enemies to get emotional and make mistakes. Stay focused and try not to let the dragon control the flow of battle.

RED DRAGON

☠ 3-5

SPECIAL POWERS

VOLCANIC ACTIVITY
Older red dragons can make the ground shake with their roar or summon spouts of burning magma from beneath the earth. Losing in a battle against a red dragon means being burned alive or crushed beneath giant steaming rocks.

FIRE BREATH
Red dragons exhale gouts of deadly flame from deep within their bodies. The heat generated can easily melt flesh and burn clothes and even armor.

Red dragons are the most greedy and vain of all the evil chromatic dragons. They gather huge treasure hoards and possess huge egos to match. They remember every item they've plundered and can recall every foe who dared to stand against them.

Arrogant, possessive, and sometimes quite impulsive, red dragons prove their superiority by gathering information on enemies before striking with ruthless fury. They see themselves as the kings of dragonkind, with lesser dragons and all other creatures as mere slaves for them to command.

LAIR Red dragons frequently build lairs in mountains or hills, sometimes within deep mines or former dwarven strongholds. Volcanic caves are the most prized by red dragons, as these provide warm gasses that the reptiles find enjoyable and add protection against any intruders foolish enough to trespass.

Unnatural earthquakes may occur in the area around the lair of an older red dragon. Sources of water tend to be warmer than normal and may even be contaminated by sulfur.

DO THIS

Watch out for tremors! If you feel the earth shaking, you may be getting close to a red dragon's lair!

Flatter them. Red dragons have tremendous egos. If you get caught by a red dragon, heaping praise on them might give you extra time needed to devise an escape plan!

DON'T DO THIS

Don't get burned. Red dragons are creatures of fire. Confronting one means you'd better be prepared, with lots of armor and protective magic to keep from getting burned.

Don't steal! Red dragons are obsessed with their treasure hoards and will hunt thieves to the ends of the earth. If you take something that's theirs, you better know what you're doing!

LEGENDARY DRAGON

☠ EPIC

TIAMAT, THE QUEEN OF EVIL DRAGONS

LAIR Tiamat lives in Avernus, a desolate dimension of war where devils battle each other in forsaken lands while fiery comets streak through the sky. In this foreboding realm stands Tiamat's temple, which has five separate spires—one for each evil dragon color.

Despite her incredible power, Tiamat is trapped in Avernus by an ancient curse. Her many followers strive to break the curse and set her free, so she may destroy all who oppose her. If they succeed, no one is safe!

iamat is the legendary and terrifying Queen of Evil Dragons. Her five heads, one for each of the evil dragon types, all share the same mind and have the same goal—to rule over all creatures and mortals, bringing about an apocalyptic Age of Dragons that would plunge the world into destructive chaos.

A regular dragon is one of the most terrifying opponents an adventurer can ever face, and Tiamat terrifies even other dragons. Just being in her presence can be enough to send most heroes running away screaming. Only the most courageous or foolhardy would ever fight the dragon queen and hope to succeed.

FIGHTING TIAMAT

Tiamat is a massive multiheaded dragon with huge wings, powerful claws, and a vicious stinging tail. She cannot be hurt by non-magical weapons, and heals quickly from damage. Her five heads can each unleash a deadly breath weapon based on its dragon type.

Black: Burning acid sprays

Blue: Crackling lightning bolts

Green: Poisonous gas clouds

Red: Gouts of burning fire

White: Freezing ice blasts

Tiamat is one of the most dangerous creatures in all of existence. She is ancient, cunning, powerful, and merciless. Defeating the Queen of Evil Dragons would take an incredible amount of power or an army, or both.

SIZE

Tiamat is approximately sixty feet long, which means she's one-third longer and taller than even the largest ancient chromatic dragon.

USING MONSTERS
TO TELL YOUR OWN STORIES

"Get ready, Boo!"

Boo the hamster squee'ed in a manner that made it abundantly clear he was not ready and probably never would be.

"Bones behind us and water below, it's time to jump!"

Minsc bombastically leapt off the top of the tower as the arrows of undead archers zipped past his face and skeletal hands grasped his tattered cloak.

As gravity quick took hold and they started to plummet toward the waves, the legendary ranger wondered if he'd make it back to Baldur's Gate in time for breakfast.

Reading about monsters kick-starts your imagination, doesn't it? With each entry, with every illustration, you start to create little stories in your mind. What happened before, what happens right after? These questions create an exciting daydream that can't stay contained.

All those wandering thoughts about action and adventure, they're the perfect way to begin building your own stories!

Your idea might start with a monster, but it can go *anywhere*: the creature's lair, the village nearby, cities and dungeons, caverns or skyscapes. You get to choose all the ingredients and stir them together. To help you as you develop your story, here are some questions to keep in mind:

WHO ARE YOUR CHARACTERS?

- Are your heroes like you or different? Young or old, human or something else? Think about the foes you must face. Great heroes require great challenges. What makes your villains memorable and powerful, and what brings them into conflict with your adventurers?

WHERE DOES YOUR STORY TAKE PLACE?

- At the top of a mountain, in a serene forest, deep underwater, or in a creepy boneyard?

WHEN DOES THE STORY HAPPEN?

- At night or during the day, in the middle of a thunderstorm or right before the bells toll to ring in the new year? Think about time passing as your story unfolds.

HOW DO THINGS CHANGE AS THE STORY PROCEEDS?

- Do your heroes succeed or fail? Do they find somewhere new or explore someplace old?

WHAT SHOULD SOMEONE FEEL AS THEY EXPERIENCE YOUR STORY?

- Do you want them to laugh or get scared? Cheer or be grossed out?

WHY ARE YOUR HEROES GOING ON THIS ADVENTURE?

- Knowing what their goals are will help you create a compelling tale of heroism and exploration.

Remember, you don't have to answer all these questions by yourself! DUNGEONS & DRAGONS is a collaborative game where you work with your friends to create your own stories. One person acts as a narrator, called a Dungeon Master, and the other players each take on the role of a hero, called a Player Character, in the adventuring party in a story. The Dungeon Master sets up a scene by describing a place and any threats that may exist, and then each player contributes ideas by explaining their own character's actions. With each scene created by the group, the story moves forward in unexpected and entertaining ways.

If you don't feel confident starting from scratch, you can go to your local gaming store and play a DUNGEONS & DRAGONS demonstration session. Demos can be a quick way to learn how the game is played and an opportunity to possibly make some brand-new friends at the same time.

After you've read through all the creatures in this little monster manual, there's even more DUNGEONS & DRAGONS material to ignite your imagination, the *Warriors & Weapons* guide is packed with character ideas and equipment to outfit your courageous adventurer. You know what dangers lurk in the darkness, now figure out who your hero will be and *fight them back*!

Published in the United States by Ten Speed Press, an imprint of Random House, a division of Penguin Random House LLC, New York.
www.crownpublishing.com
www.tenspeed.com

Ten Speed Press and the Ten Speed Press colophon are registered trademarks of Penguin Random House LLC.

Library of Congress Cataloging-in-Publication Data
Names: Zub, Jim, author. | Conceptopolis, illustrator.
Title: Monsters & creatures : a young adventurer's guide / written by Jim
  Zub, with Stacy King and Andrew Wheeler ; illustrations by Conceptopolis.
Other titles: Monsters and creatures
Description: First edition. | New York : Ten Speed Press, [2019] | Series:
  Dungeons & dragons young adventurer's guides | Includes index. | Audience:
  Age 8-12. | Audience: Grade 4 to 6.
Identifiers: LCCN 2018050270 | ISBN 9781984856401 (hardback) |
  ISBN 9781984856418 (ebook)
Subjects: LCSH: Dungeons and dragons (Game)—Handbooks, manuals,
  etc.—Juvenile literature. | Dungeons and dragons (Game)—Pictorial
  works—Juvenile literature. | BISAC: JUVENILE NONFICTION / Games &
  Activities / General. | GAMES / Role Playing & Fantasy. | JUVENILE
  NONFICTION / Media Tie-In.
Classification: LCC GV1469.62.D84 Z836 2019 | DDC 793.93—dc23
LC record available at https://lccn.loc.gov/2018050270

Hardcover ISBN: 978-1-9848-5640-1
eBook ISBN: 978-1-9848-5641-8

Printed in China

Publisher: Aaron Wehner
Art Director and Designer: Betsy Stromberg
Editors: Patrick Barb and Julie Bennett
Managing Editor: Doug Ogan
Production Designer: Lisa Bieser
Wizards of the Coast Team: David Gershman, Kate Irwin, Adam Lee, Hilary Ross, Liz Schuh
Illustrations: Conceptopolis, LLC

10 9 8 7 6 5

First Edition